Etsy Business Success For Beginners:

Build a Successful Etsy Business Empire with Proven Etsy Shop Building Tactics, SEO tricks, Social Media Strategies, Product Selection and Pricing Tips

By

Dale Blake

Table of Contents

Etsy Business Success For Beginners: Build a Successful Etsy Business Empire with Proven Etsy Shop Building Tactics, SEO tricks, Social Media Strategies, Product Selection and Pricing Tips

By Dale Blake

First Published, 2014

Printed in the United States of America

Introduction

ETSY is a name not new for online shoppers and sellers. It is a global marketplace for handmade goods and craft supplies which encourages people from all over the world to sell their products online and earn some money while sitting at their home.

With a site like ETSY, it is easy to start your own business. The site provides people an opportunity to access millions of buyers worldwide and to sell products online without any hassle. Since 2005, thousands of people are benefiting from ETSY. They are using ETSY as a platform where they can showcase their creativity and make a living from it.

Chapter 1. Why to Sell on ETSY?

ETSY offers numerous benefits which may not be possible when you build your own ecommerce website.

Tests your ability

ETSY is a great place to start your business and test your ability. It will help you assess your potential. You will gradually understand the areas where you lack and the things you need to improve. The experience on ETSY will help you immensely if you ever think of starting you own ecommerce website. It will also aid you in building a temperament required to run a business.

Expands your reach

It is difficult to access your potential customers with your own website but on ETSY, it is not difficult to reach millions of buyers and to introduce yourself and your products.

Showcases your creativity

ETSY is a platform which anyone can use to express his creativity. You can sell anything on ETSY which you have designed using your imagination and you want the world to see it and appreciate it. What more you can ask for, earning money with the things you have created with love and dedication.

Requires little investment

You can start your business on ETSY on either large or small scale depending on how much you can invest in your business. But obviously, you must have something to sell whether it is homemade product or a vintage item.

Chapter 2. How to Get Started on ETSY?

The process of starting your business on ETSY is fairly easy. All you need is an online shop on ETSY and a product to start you work. For setting up a shop or to creating an account on ETSY, you need to follow these steps.

Make yourself familiar with ETSY rules and policies

Before you set up a shop on ETSY, it is advisable to go through ETSY rules and policies. You can read the seller guideline available on ETSY website to get complete information about selling rules and regulations.

Knowing rules and policies is imperative to avoid mistakes. If any item does not comply or is inconsistent with the policies of ETSY, it will be removed from the shop.

Decide what to sell on ETSY

First of all, you need to decide what you want to sell on ETSY. There are three main categories to choose from: handmade good, vintage items and craft supplies.

1. Handmade goods

From clothing to jewelry to toys, you can sell any type of handmade good on ETSY. But the product should be either created by the seller himself or the other members of the shop. ETSY does not allow reselling of the products and to maintain genuineness, ETSY asks shop owners to list the names of all the members in your shop involved in making of the product.

2. Vintage items

Vintage item can be another option from selling perspective. But if you want to sell a vintage item, it has to be at least 20 years old. The piece should be worthy to sell and be in good condition.

3. Craft Supplies

Craft supplies may include ribbons, glitters, gift wrapping papers, beads, crystal jars or bottles etc. These supplies are basically raw materials required to make DIY sort of projects.

If you not sure what to sell on ETSY, you can browse through existing shops to get an idea about the products. You can also use an app named Craftcount to find out the top sellers on ETSY, top homemade products, top vintage items and top craft supplies. Craftcount will give you a clear idea about what kind of products other sellers are having in their shops and what kind of products are in demand.

Products you cannot sell on ETSY

You can sell anything on ETSY except:

Alcoholic beverages

Weapons

Drugs

Tobacco

Live animals

Animal bones

Human remains

Explosive material

Motor vehicles

Porn stuff

Hatred based material

What ETSY charges for becoming one of its members?

There are no charges for creating an account or setting up a shop on ETSY. Plus, you do not need to pay any monthly fees to retain your membership.

ETSY will charge $0.20 for listing each item or product. The listings have to be renewed after every four months or after products are sold.

ETSY charges 3.5% on every sold item.

ETSY will charge additional fees, if a seller uses ETSY promotional tools for the advertising of his products.

ETSY also charges shipping fees. But fees will vary depending on the place where the product is made and the destination where the product will be sent.

How to create an ETSY account?

Go to ETSY website. You will find the "Register" button on the right of their home page. Click it and enter your name, email, password and username. If you want to receive ETSY newsletter or alerts, you can tick mark the option placed in the bottom of the page. Now your ETSY shop is opened and ready to make money.

Choose a name for your shop

You need to pick a name for your ETSY shop. Your shop name will be your identity on ETSY. So the shop name has to be attractive, distinguishable and easy to remember. It has to be something which standout from the rest of the crowd.

Before deciding a name, it is necessary to make sure that anything similar is not already used by someone else. Your buyers do not get confused with the similarity of the names.

Keep the name short and catchy.

Choose a name which reflects your product and its features. If you are selling multiple kind of products on your shop, then it better to choose a name that is suitable for multiple types of products.

You also need to add a shop title beneath the shop name. The title has to be precise which can sums up the qualities of your shop or product.

Write your profile

Profile is something which describes your personality. On ETSY, you also need a profile to introduce yourself to a buyer or ETSY community. You need to tell who you are, what your interests and hobbies are, what are the characteristics that sets you apart from other shops or anything similar to that.

Your profile has to be simple and concise yet attractive for the readers. It has to be written in conversational tone but should be devoid of fictional touches and should be professional enough to help build a trust on you and your products.

The profile can be comprised of single paragraph or can be break down to multiple paragraphs if necessary.

If you own multiple shops on ETSY, you can include the links of all those shops. You can also provide the addresses of your social networking sites to share pictures or information with your potential buyers.

Shop Policies

Sellers are required to list their shop policies. You may include payment methods, shipping details, refund and exchange policies and FAQS. For instance, describe what is your policy regarding return and exchange? Can a buyer return or exchange a product if he is not satisfied with it? If yes, than in what time frame a product can be returned?

All your policies must be consistent with the rules and policies of ETSY.

Create a banner

Banner is probably the first thing your prospective buyer sees on your shop. So it has to be eye catching and appealing, something which can instantly grab the attention of whoever sees it.

ETSY has certain requirement regarding a banner. The banner has to be exactly 760 pixels wide and 100 pixels in length.

You can either made a banner by your own or use ETSY Banner Generator tool to create a banner for your shop. The tool is free and it will provide you designs, font styles and colors that you need to customize your shop banner.

Add a profile picture

You should have a profile image on ETSY. The image must be:

75 x 75 in size

Square in shape

You can replace your image with another one any time. Having a profile image is optional; you can leave the space blank as well. However having a profile picture can definitely help you to make more sales.

Add location

Add your location, your city, the province and the country where you belong.

Add shop announcement

Add shop announcement is the section where you enter the details about your shop. It can include the features of your products or any latest information about your product which you want to share with your buyers.

It can be just one paragraph or multiple paragraphs or sentences followed by opening paragraph, depending how much space you require to summarize your topic.

Chapter 3. How to List Your Items?

First of all you need to fill "About this item" section. Enter the answers of these questions who made it, what kind of item it is, and when it was made.

Then scroll down and categorize your product. You will be provided a list of products. Enter your product in the relevant section.

Select item types. There are two options available, physical item and digital file. Mark your item type by pressing any of the buttons.

If your product has variations then you need to enter this as well. The variations may include size, color, height, length, material etc. Enter the relevant information in the section.

Then add photographs of your item. You will have five spaces for each listing. Try to utilize all five of the spaces by adding different angles of your products.

The image of a product has to be not more than 1000 pixels in width and 1000 pixels in height. The more a photograph is detailed and clear, the more it will be attractive for the buyers and helps them in making their buying decisions.

Item title

Add a descriptive title which can tell the reader a bit about your item. A title can be up to 140 characters. Keep it simple and professional. Plus, include those words that are more searchable regarding your product so your prospective customers can easily access your shop they type relevant words.

Description of the item

Providing a description of the product is as important as anything else. But the description has to be concise and compact that can give a clear idea of the product.

Make sure to include general features of the product. For instance, if you are selling clothes then write down the sizes, what material is used for making it, how many colors are available and what is the price of a dress. If your dress has some unique features, then do not forget to highlight them as well.

Optimize your description

When you write a description, tag them with keyword. It will allow the buyers to easily access the product they are looking for.

You can add up to 13 tags. The tags will serve similar kind of purpose as general Search Engine Optimization. Shoppers enter words on browser window. Results will show up when words are entered so think like a shopper and use those keywords as tags which are closely linked to your products.

Enter price, quantity and shipping information

Next, you need to fill price, quantity and shipping info application. For instance, your shipping info may include the time frame when a product will reach to its destination, the country that you are shipping from and the country from where the product will be shipped. You can ship a product either within your country or anywhere in the world.

Publish your listing

Once you have entered all the required information, your item is ready to be published and viewed publically. ETSY will charge 0.20 USD for each published listing.

You need to pay same fee if you include multiple quantities of a single product in a list. You can also add variations such as size, color or material of a dress in the same listing.

ETSY allows you to have more than one shop but to open new shop; you need to have a new username and a new email address. You cannot list exactly the same item on new shop which you have already listed in your other shop. You cannot share or transfer the same information such as review, listings etc from one shop to another.

Set your language preferences

Since ETSY is a global marketplace, it provides an opportunity to the sellers from all over the world to communicate with buyers in their own language or the language they are comfortable to speak. The language which you choose for your shop will not be changed later but you can add more languages if needed.

Choose payment methods

If you want to open a shop on ETSY, you must have a valid credit/debit card and you must set your payment method prior to selling your products so you can receive your payments without any fuss. You must select a method which is most convenient for you.

You can choose any of the following options:

Credit/debit cards

You can receive your payment through credit/debit card. These cards may include Visa, MasterCard, and American Express etc. This is the method which ensures safe and easy transactions. ETSY will process the payments, deposit it your bank account and you will receive payment in your local currency.

Check/Money order

ETSY also offers conventional methods of transferring money such as personal check or money order. If you choose one of these options, you need to provide your valid mailing address so your buyer can send you your payments.

PayPal

PayPal is a popular payment method on ETSY and payment can be instantly transferred to your PayPal account. But payments will not be sent on your personal PayPal account. You need to open premier or business PayPal account for this purpose.

ETSY gift cards

You can also receive your payment in the form of ETSY gift cards. All you need is to sign up ETSY's Direct Checkout option to avail this facility.

Chapter 4. How to Market Your Shop?

ETSY is place crowded with thousands of shops. Your shop will lost in the marketplace if you do not use promotional tools or run advertising campaigns. If you want to get success on ETSY, these are the few things which can be done to make your shop visible and to boost your sales.

Use ETSY advertising tools

A seller can promote his products by using ETSY promotional tools. You can either choose CPC or you set a budget for displaying your listings.

When you purchase an Ad, it will be displayed on ETSY website and the payment will be on Cost-Per-Click basis. It means ETSY will not charge you for providing space on the website; you will pay only when a shopper clicks your Ad.

If you cannot afford it, you can fix an amount and ETSY will display your listings depending on the fixed amount and seller will receive the billings on monthly basis.

Social media marketing

Every seller needs social media presence to generate traffic and eventually to drive sales. If you market your ETSY shop on social networking sites such as Facebook and Twitter, it will not only make your shop visible but will help you increase your sales as well.

You can write information about ETSY products on your Facebook and Twitter and upload the photographs of the products. Your sales will also improve when people will discuss and share the information and photographs in their social circle.

Utilize your own ecommerce website to promote of ETSY shop

Many of the ETSY sellers have their own ecommerce website as well. If you own such a website, then use it for the promotion of your ETSY shop. You can also do it other way around. In both cases, you will the one who get the benefits.

How to price your product or item?

For having a clear idea about the prices of the products, search Google or visit ETSY shops. Do not price a product neither too high so it will go beyond the reach of a customer nor too low that customers start to think that your product is of low quality.

The price structure should be appealing yet affordable for the buyers. It also offers a sufficient enough profit margin which is fair to yourself and to the hard work and effort you put in creating a product.

Some customers try to bargain with the seller and offer a low price for buying a product. It is up to you deal with this situation. You can sell a product on a low price offered by the customer or tell them that prices are firm and there is no margin of negotiations.

Chapter 5. Tips to Become a Successful Seller on ETSY

Creating an account and setting up a shop on ETSY is just a starting point. Becoming a successful ETSY seller has to be the ultimate goal. To achieve this purpose, you need to keep in mind the following tips.

Do market research

Doing market research is the first step for having a successful business on ETSY. Look at the other ETSY shops that are successful and selling the same products which you are planning to sell. Figure out why they are successful. What are the things they do to increase their sale.

Also, look into those websites that are doing not too well on ETSY. You can learn many things from them as well. Find out the reasons why they are not successful. Avoid those mistakes and utilize best practices.

Your product has to be unique in some way

You product must have uniqueness in it if you want to sell it on ETSY. It must reflect your personality and your creativity and anything else which can set your product apart from others. This tip is applicable only on homemade goods not on the vintage item because a vintage item is itself a unique thing.

Stay connected with other shop owners or ETSY community

Once you register yourself as an ETSY seller, join and participate in site's forums. Stay connected with other owners, discuss your ideas and share your experiences with them. Talk to the successful sellers and ask for advices or helpful tips. You will also remain updated about latest happenings in ETSY if you communicate with other owners.

Highlight your products with high-quality photography

Since ETSY shops are virtual, buyers can not view a product live. So it is up to you how you present your product on your web shop.

Only add those photographs that highlight your product clearly. Make sure to use a quality camera and a professional photographer if you are not satisfied with your own results. A good photograph with clear image of the product will help immensely your customers in making their buying decisions.

Keep search engine optimization factor in your mind

How can you imagine increasing your sales if your prospective customers will not reach to your shop? Many of the customers find a shop through search engines. So it is imperative to tag most relevant keywords. Every time when a shopper will enters words relevant to your product, your shop will appear on search results.

Build good relationship with buyers

Having good relationship is necessary not only for a successful ETSY business but for any business. Respect your customers and talk with them generously. Try to respond their queries and feedback a quickly as possible. Respect their opinion about your product and try to improve it in the light of their suggestions.

Offer a great buying experience to your customers

Try to provide your customers a convenient buying experience. Keep your return or exchange policies. Make shipping and payment method as much convenient as possible. Do not limit your product to a single country. Try to expand it and ship products to multiple countries.

If your customer had a great buying experience on your shop, he/she will definitely come back to your shop again and again.

Offer incentives to your customers

Offering incentives or special deals is a great way to attract more and more buyers. By offering incentives you can turn occasional customers into loyal customers because discounts and deals will force them to buy products from your shop over and over again. A sale on you products such as 10% off on dress for a specific period is the most common incentive a seller can offer to his customer.

Have a great packaging

Packaging of a product may not seem an important issue but the fact is it plays a vital role in building a positive image of a seller. Great packaging will make your buyer realize how much you care about your customers.

You can use colorful ribbons, wrapping papers, stickers and beautiful boxes depending on the product you are selling.

You can also consider writing personalized messages and attach it with the product. These kinds of small things can have a magical effect on your sales.

Provide newsletter to keep shoppers updated

You can create your own newsletter on ETSY. A newsletter is something which makes people updated about your latest products. You can either directly send newsletter to your customers or encourage them to subscribe it. You can provide a link to your newsletter subscription on your ETSY's About Page and your social networking sites such as Facebook, Twitter. The shopper, who wants to hear from you, will subscribe this service and will likely be take interest in buying your product.

Use proper channels for advertising of your product

Utilize different channels to advertise your product and to boost your sales. Social networking sites can prove helpful in this regard. You can add your product description along with the photos of your product on social networking sites. Within seconds, hundreds of people will get aware of your products and will share them with their friends if they find your products interesting and worthy to bought.

Use ETSY apps to manage your shop 24/7

ETSY offers an app called "Sell on ETSY" to manage your shop from a smartphone or tablet which means you can control your shop from anywhere whether you are in your office and at home. The app allows a seller deal with their buyers, process orders and updates the listings anytime.

If you download this app, ETSY will send you a notification or alert every time you receive a message from buyers. Prompt replying to the customer will boost your brand reputation and help you in running a successful shop on ETSY.

Final Words

ETSY is a large, crowded marketplace and is one of the best platforms to express your creativity and to earn some money by selling products designed and created by you. But making a name for yourself here is not so easy. If you want to run a shop successfully on ETSY, you should be aware of rules, policies, dos and don'ts and the functioning of the website.

You should remember that it takes time to become a successful seller on ETSY. So you need to have patience, guts and plans to overcome the challenges which will come along the way. Initially, it will be a bit difficult to sell your items but you can make your product visible by using advertising tools and other appropriate tactics and there will be a time when you start to achieve your milestones. Moreover, you will learn many things from this platform which will help you a lot when you set up your own business on a larger scale.

I want to personally thank you for reading my book. I hope you found information in this book useful and I would be very grateful if you could leave your honest review about this book. I certainly want to thank you in advance for doing this.

If you have the time, you can check my other books too.